HOW
BE MORE
AWESOME:
THE STUDENT
PLANNER EDITION

**A practical journey to
support your resilience
and grit, alongside
a handy academic year
diary, helpful 'to do' lists
and exercises.**

Name: _Elliot Preece_

If lost, please return to: _____

Thanks for caring!

Please add your favourite quote/ fact/ joke:

_____

_____

"The Awesome journal helps me think
and reflect about the good things in my day
and friendships. It's full of tasks and
challenges that help me face day to day life"

Liverpool Studio School student

"A wonderful book and resource"

Sir Anthony Seldon,
former Master of Wellington College;
Vice Chancellor of Buckingham University
and co-Founder of Action for Happiness

Welcome

Welcome to How to be More Awesome: the student planner edition. This is a revision of our original How to be More Awesome journal and now includes a 28-day starter wellbeing programme; a week-to-view student planner and a structured 38-week resilience and strength-focused support programme. This edition is a personal wellbeing and resilience programme, created within the framework of an academic year diary.

These changes were suggested by students and teachers at the Studio Liverpool, part of the Northern Schools Trust, based on their experience of using the original How to be More Awesome journal. The marketing, sales and distribution of this version will be managed and delivered as part of the Studio Liverpool entrepreneurship programme.

All human beings are 'awesome' at some level – we all have talents, skills and strengths. The challenge for all of us is to maximise their use and build on their foundations. Positive Psychology research indicates that positive emotions, encouraging wellbeing and gratitude promotes creativity, achievement, and builds personal resilience – which helps your ability to deal with the tough times. This journal draws from Positive Psychology and its cousin Appreciative Inquiry, creating a personal development tool that can:

★ Help you work from your strengths and what you're good at;

★ Build your 'bounce-back ability' (resilience);

★ Help you value and enjoy the people and environment around you (appreciate);

★ Support you to think about and design the future you want (inquire);

★ Help you think more about what you do (reflect)

★ Build your confidence and health (wellbeing)

More explanation on the words in brackets, Appreciative Inquiry and other influences is available in the guidance section on page 155.

Contents

The journal is set out in a number of parts:

★ a 28 day wellbeing programme;

★ a week-to-view diary covering an academic year

★ a schedule of exercises and guidance on how to use it, providing information on how to reach your more 'awesome' self.

This journal and workbook will help you build on your existing strengths and what you do well. Use it to explore ways you can build stronger relationships, organise yourself to learn more effectively and develop your 'bounce-back ability'.

We hope you enjoy the experience and have fun on the way – it's up to you.

Impact review

Feedback on the original journal included the need for tools and guidelines to help review the impact of using Awesome on students. In collaboration with the Studio School, Appreciating People has co-designed an Appreciative Inquiry-based review and impact tool, which is available from the Studio, Liverpool, alongside information and guidance on its use. A short training course will be also available to help teachers maximise its use – you'll find contact details in the guidance section.

∞ PART ONE ∞
What is journaling and how can it help?
Why writing it down is important...

The word 'journaling' comes from the word 'journey'. Writing and using a journal is a personal thing and should be seen as being a confidential process. Sharing information about the experience (rather than the content) is a great educational and learning opportunity. Many of the exercises and tasks can be shared and used to chart people's progress. The important thing is that this needs to be part of a personal decision and can be supported by an agreed contract with a friend/teacher/mentor.

Journaling is an ancient tradition. Throughout history, people have kept journals and diaries – they've made a rich contribution to our understanding of history. There is increasing research to support the idea that journaling has a positive effect on personal wellbeing and provides a range of unexpected benefits.* The act of writing accesses the left brain, which is analytical and rational. While your left brain is occupied, your right brain is free to create, be intuitive and feel. Recording things in your journal can help remove mental blocks. It allows you to use all your brain power and strengths to better understand yourself, others and the world around you.

Journaling has a number of benefits:

1. It helps you clarify your thoughts – taking a few moments to write down ideas can help you sort out the jumble of thoughts inside your brain.

2. Helps know yourself better. Observing and writing regularly helps you get to know what makes you feel happy and confident, appreciate yourself, connect with your strengths, provide a clear view on situations and actions you're thinking of taking and people you may have to deal with. All of these are important for your emotional wellbeing...

3. Helps to reduce stress – writing about things that upset and challenge you helps to release these feelings, so you will feel calmer and better able to cope.

4. Helps solve problems more effectively – typically we solve problems via a left brain analytical perspective, but sometimes the problem can only be solved by engaging right-brained creativity and intuition. Writing about and recording (including drawing, sketching etc) thoughts unlocks those abilities, providing the opportunity for unexpected solutions to arise.

5. Helps resolve disagreements with others. Writing and recording about misunderstandings, concerns and issues can avoid stewing about the matter. It will help you understand different views and contribute to a resolution.

6. Allows you to track patterns, trends, improvements, and personal development over a period of time.

* Purcell, M. (2006): *The Health Benefits of Journaling* in *Psych Central*. Retrieved on June 25, 2014, from http://psychcentral.com/lib/the-health-benefits-of-journaling/000721

Appreciative journaling adds another dimension to journaling. It's about actively seeking the good side of a situation and seeing how we can expand on that. We're not asking you to ignore or whitewash difficult situations or experiences – but rather than 'ruminating' and wasting energy on things which increase your negative emotions, search out and focus on positive ones**. What we put our attention on grows in our minds.** Ruminating is the name we give to focusing on negative thoughts – it's like a record that's stuck and keeps repeating the same lines; for example, replaying an argument with a friend in your head. Research has shown that rumination is associated with a variety of negative consequences; appreciative journaling is a very helpful alternative.

Sharing experiences and the online community

If you find journaling a positive step, we'd love it if you shared your experiences. We've created a Twitter hashtag, #beingmoreawesome and a web site www.bemoreawesome.net to encourage you to share your journaling experiences. The site provides easy access to the links highlighted in the journal and extra resources, including training guidance.

∾ PART TWO ∾
Helpful hints to get going and useful information

Helpful hints

As we've already stated, keeping a journal takes time and practice and it's likely that you'll stop and start a number of times. That's fine, and to be expected. But if you keep persevering it will get easier – habits develop with practice.

To help you, we've provided a 28-day starter programme plus an exercise menu to choose from. The easier exercises are at the beginning and, as you'll see, some of them are repeated – this helps develop your 'appreciative muscle'*. You don't have to do the 28 days in sequence; our experience has indicated people like a choice and some people will prefer to start by drawing from the exercise menu.

So how does this all work? Put simply, to get different results in your life, you need to try doing some things differently. What you do is changed by thinking different thoughts, imagining different behaviour, changing existing beliefs that limit your possible options, and becoming more aware of how your emotions influence what you do.

*Developing an appreciative muscle is like physical fitness – it takes training, practice, and repetition.

Good luck, enjoy it and note the difference – have fun!

Useful guidance

★ Start with the 28-day programme to help build your confidence – aim to do one exercise a day

★ Find the best time for you to do the work – it can be morning, last thing at night or at lunchtime. It just needs to be whatever works best for you...

★ Use mind maps, spidergrams, sketches, doodles, or cut and paste images – any process that helps you feel creative and express yourself

★ Always start with small and tiny contributions – the bigger things will follow

★ Starting and stopping is fine. It gets easier with practice and can be hard at first – be persistent

★ If you feel negative, that's OK. Try and flip it by considering questions like 'what can I learn here?' and 'what do I need to do differently?'

★ Remember that dreams, future plans and thoughts are the reasons we get things done

★ Thinking time – often called reflection – is essential both for wellbeing and being more effective

★ Try using social media to share observations and thoughts with friends and colleagues

You will also see that there are jokes, fun facts and quotations... they're there to make you smile and think. Enjoy!

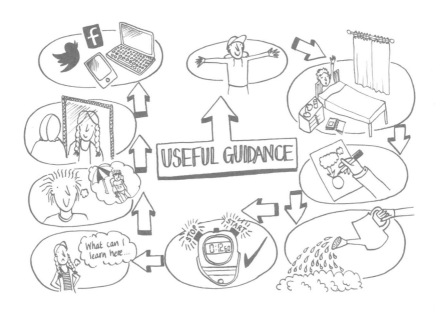

Task 1

Personal SOAR™

SOAR™ (**S**trengths, **O**pportunities, **A**spirations and **R**esults/ **R**esources) is an alternative to a SWOT analysis (**S**trengths, **W**eaknesses, **O**pportunities and **T**hreats). A SWOT analysis is traditionally used with organisations and planning tasks. While it's great for undertaking practical tasks like building a bridge, threats and weaknesses tend to dominate the response; it is not visionary and does not suggest measurements of success. Both SOAR™ and SWOT are used in personal development – the question is would you rather SWOT or help yourself SOAR™?

Using the blank table on the next page, create a personal SOAR™ using the questions in the table below as a guide. Use either bullet points or images – it's up to you. Sometimes it helps to do the aspirations before the opportunities. You will review this SOAR™ towards the end of the journal...

Strengths

★ *What are you good at – your skills and strengths?*

★ *What do your friends and family think you are good at?*

★ *What special knowledge do you have?*

Opportunities

★ *List the opportunities out there for you*

★ *Consider what opportunities can help build your skills and strengths*

★ *Consider how you can utilise the skills and strengths you have*

Aspirations

★ *What is your passion?*

★ *What do you want to do and achieve?*

★ *What would it look like if you had already achieved it?*

Resources/Results*

★ *What resources do you need to meet your aspirations and maximise your opportunities?*

★ *What are the first two things you need to do?*

★ *How would you know you have achieved anything and how would you measure success?*

★ *In what ways would you celebrate your achievements?*

* ***You can use either or both***

Your personal SOAR™

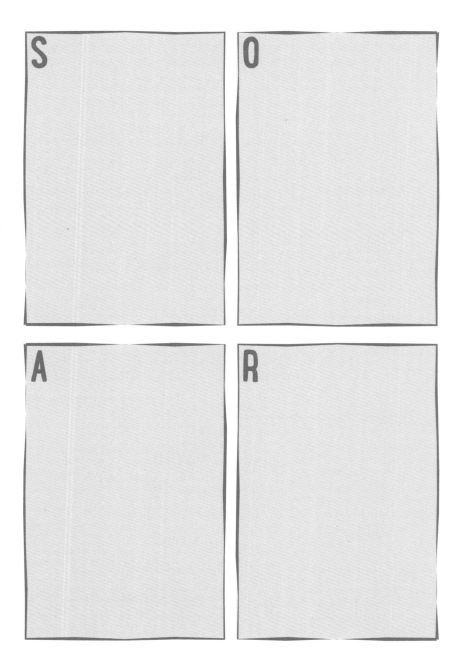

S

O

A

R

Being better organised - useful ideas

In the development process one of the students requested some helpful hints and guidance for being better organised. Here are ten suggestions:

★ Firstly, don't panic - you're not alone... All of us would like to be better organised!

★ 'To do' lists are a great start as they let you clear your head of all the things you're trying to remember. Just try to make sure they're not too long, so you don't get overwhelmed.

★ Try and resist doing the things you really enjoy first - it often means you avoid the important ones. Sometimes start with the worst job or task, as when it's done you'll get a sense of relief.

★ Often being organised is about thinking ahead - getting things ready the night before. A useful quote to remember is 'it's not about the plan - it's about the planning' (General Dwight Eisenhower, Commander, D Day).

★ Use a diary or an online calendar to plan ahead - there are lots of apps like Trello that can help you organise tasks.

★ Remember - things normally take longer than you planned.

★ Be aware of text and e-mail addiction. Try limiting your replies to once an hour if you're busy. And always read through carefully before pressing 'send'...

★ 'Back planning' is great. This is when you work back from the desired success or achievement and plan through the stages you had to go through to get there.

★ On occasions, being organised can be about stopping and thinking - go for a walk...

★ Try and operate with less clutter

★ Work at the time that best suits you. Most people are freshest in the morning and dip after lunch, so tackle the most creative or challenging tasks in the morning.

★ Urgent AND important? Draw yourself a grid with URGENT/ NOT URGENT on one side and IMPORTANT/ NOT IMPORTANT on the other axis. Allocate your tasks with an x on the grid, according to how important/ urgent etc. they are. Concentrate on working through the tasks that are both urgent AND important first - those that are neither urgent nor important should be last on your list...

Using these suggestions will also promote your wellbeing and effectiveness

'To do' list tips

Creating and using 'to do' lists are a helpful and practical way to be better organised, create a sense of achievement and plan better – all of which contribute to your wellbeing. Below are some helpful hints and a template:

★ Keep your list short and break down the tasks into 'bite-sized chunks'

★ Ideally a task should not take more than one to two hours to achieve – if it does break it down into sub-tasks

★ Try using the term 'have done' list as a way of changing your mindset

★ Once you're comfortable using 'to do' lists you can start differentiating between urgency and importance – it's practice!

★ Think about creating separate lists for personal and work/ college/ school

★ Consider this quotation 'it's about first doing what is essential, then desirable, followed by "it's nice if you have time"' (Helen Bush)

★ Prioritise the tasks from A = very urgent to F = unimportant

★ You can use your 'to do' list to create a list of challenges and dreams about things you want to do.

Example of a 'to do' list

Task/ Activity	Priority (A to F, where A = very important and F = unimportant

❧ PART THREE ❧
Getting started – a 28-day wellbeing programme

This section contains a 28-day programme with a 'day-to-view', including a task called 'three good things', for you to do every day. Positive psychology research tells us that repeating this exercise for 20 days or more has a positive personal impact.

Every five days we've also included a 'to do' list, to help you with your planning and organising. At the end of each seven-day cycle there's space for a parent, teacher or coach signature and comments. This is a good way to review and mark progress. On your weekends, you can also try some of the exercises from the menu, like the stone balancing one.

At both the half way and end points of the programme are opportunities for journaling, plus some pages with more exercises and others blank, so that you can choose from the exercise menu. At the end of the 28-day programme, you'll find a review and reflect exercise. You can also pick an exercise from the menu on page 148.

Day one to day five

Three good things*

For five days, write down three good things that happened to you on each day. They can be small – like *I answered a really hard question in class/ query at work* or big, like *I got a top grade for my work/ got a new job*. Against each positive event, write:

★ Why did this good thing happen?

★ What does it mean to me?

★ How can I have more of it?

Adapted from the Penn State University PRP (Penn Resilience Programme) for US schools

Monday

Three good things

Tuesday

Three good things

Wednesday

Three good things

Thursday

Three good things

Friday

Three good things

Saturday

Sunday

Caring about happiness does not mean ignoring sadness or pretending everything is fine. It's about getting the best out of whatever life brings
ANON

Parent signature

Comments

Teacher/coach signature

'To do' list

Task/ Activity	Priority (A to F, where A = very important and F = unimportant)

Monday

Three good things

Tuesday

Three good things

Wednesday

Three good things

Thursday

Three good things

Friday

Three good things

Saturday

Sunday

Act as if what you do makes a difference – it does
WILLIAM JAMES

Parent signature

Comments

Teacher/coach signature

'To do' list

Task/ Activity	Priority (A to F, where A = very important and F = unimportant

Monday

Three good things

Tuesday

Three good things

Wednesday  Three good things

Thursday

Three good things

Friday

Three good things

Saturday

Sunday

Imagination is more important than knowledge
ALBERT EINSTEIN

Parent signature

Comments

Teacher/coach signature

33

'To do' list

Task/ Activity	Priority (A to F, where A = very important and F = unimportant

Monday

Three good things

Tuesday

Three good things

Wednesday

Three good things

Thursday

Three good things

Friday

Three good things

Saturday

Sunday

When you learn to appreciate yourself more,
then appreciating others comes more easily
ANON

_____
Parent signature

Comments

_____
Teacher/coach signature

'To do' list

Task/ Activity	Priority (A to F, where A = very important and F = unimportant

Review task

Well done – you've now completed a 28-day resilience programme. Write your answers to these questions:

1. What have you enjoyed about the process?

2. What have learned about yourself?

3. What are the changes you have noticed in yourself?

4. How has the 28-day programme helped you? (It can be a tiny thing!)

❧ PART THREE ☙
Weeks five to 38

For the next 34 weeks, we've changed the structure to a week-to-view diary, followed by a weekly exercise that can be completed individually or in groups. If you prefer, you can also replace the task with one from the task and exercise menu on page 148. Changing and adapting the exercises will often depend on what suits group needs. The important thing is to notice the ways the programme is affecting your wellbeing and thoughts.

Monday

Tuesday

Wednesday

Thursday

Friday

Saturday

Sunday

If plan A didn't work, the alphabet has
25 more letters. Stay cool!
ANON

Parent signature   Comments

Teacher/coach signature

Exercise

Try and do a new thing every day

Research shows that doing one new thing every day can help your long term wellbeing. It could be a small thing like taking a different route home and seeing how many different types of trees you can see. Make a weekly note of what they are.

'To do' list

Task/ Activity	Priority (A to F, where A = very important and F = unimportant

Monday

Tuesday

Wednesday

Thursday

Friday

Saturday

Sunday

Humans are born with 300 bones in their body, but by the time we reach adulthood we only have 206 bones. This happens because many of them join together to make a single bone...

Parent signature

Comments

Teacher/coach signature

Exercise

What are you good at? If you're not sure, what do you think your friends and/ or family think you're good at? You can always ask them!

'To do' list

Task/ Activity	Priority (A to F, where A = very important and F = unimportant

Monday

Tuesday

Wednesday

Thursday

Friday

Saturday

Sunday

It always seems impossible until it's done
NELSON MANDELA

Parent signature   Comments

Teacher/coach signature

Exercise

What new skill would you like to learn and what is the first step you'd need to do to achieve it?

'To do' list

Task/ Activity	Priority (A to F, where A = very important and F = unimportant

Monday

Tuesday

Wednesday

Thursday

Week 8

Friday

Saturday

Sunday

A typical lead pencil will draw a line 35 miles long

Parent signature

Comments

Teacher/coach signature

Exercise

When things are going wrong for you, how do you bounce back and become more resilient? Provide an example and what you did...

'To do' list

Task/ Activity	Priority (A to F, where A = very important and F = unimportant

Monday

Tuesday

Wednesday

Thursday

Friday

Saturday

Sunday

Success is walking from failure to failure
with no less enthusiasm
WINSTON S. CHURCHILL

Parent signature   Comments

Teacher/coach signature

Exercise

What are the strengths that help you when you're experiencing difficulty or a challenge?

'To do' list

Task/ Activity	Priority (A to F, where A = very important and F = unimportant

Monday

Tuesday

Wednesday

Thursday

Week 10

Friday

Saturday

Sunday

The word 'toy' comes from an old English word for 'tool'

Parent signature

Comments

Teacher/coach signature

Exercise

Think of a relationship you really value. What could you do to let this person know how special he or she is?

'To do' list

Task/ Activity	Priority (A to F, where A = very important and F = unimportant

Monday

Tuesday

Wednesday

Thursday

Friday

Saturday

Sunday

The real voyage of discovery consists not in
seeing new landscapes, but in having new eyes
MARCEL PROUST

Parent signature   Comments

Teacher/coach signature

Exercise

Think of a person who has helped you in the past but you forgot to say thanks. You might have received a gift, been given a really useful piece of advice, or had someone support you through a difficult time. Get in touch and say thank you, send them a text, or say thanks through your Facebook page.

'To do' list

Task/ Activity	Priority (A to F, where A = very important and F = unimportant

Monday

Tuesday

Wednesday

Thursday

Week 12

Friday

Saturday

Sunday

Scallops have approximately 100 eyes
around the edge of their shell ⊙⊙⊙⊙⊙⊙⊙⊙⊙⊙⊙⊙⊙⊙⊙⊙

Parent signature

Comments

Teacher/coach signature

Exercise

Think of the most creative activities you do and how you can do more of them. Draw up a list of the creative activities you do and think of one you'd like to do more of...

'To do' list

Task/ Activity	Priority (A to F, where A = very important and F = unimportant

Monday

Tuesday

Wednesday

Thursday

Friday

Saturday

Sunday

Reality leaves a lot to the imagination
JOHN LENNON

Parent signature   Comments

Teacher/coach signature

Exercise

What could you do more of this coming fortnight to take an important step forward in your life? After two weeks, take some time to reflect and then write up what you've achieved... Don't forget to check back later to see what you've achieved.

'To do' list

Task/ Activity	Priority (A to F, where A = very important and F = unimportant

Monday

Tuesday

Wednesday

Thursday

Friday

Saturday

Sunday

The smile is the most frequently used facial expression
– it can use anything from ten to 53 muscles. depending
how broad your smile is!

Parent signature

Comments

Teacher/coach signature

Exercise

Sometimes it's good to lighten up – what can you find to laugh about this week?

'To do' list

Task/ Activity	Priority (A to F, where A = very important and F = unimportant

Monday

Tuesday

Wednesday

Thursday

Friday

Saturday

Sunday

Martin Luther King did not say 'I have a strategic plan'. Instead he shouted 'I have a DREAM' and he created a crusade
ANON

Parent signature   Comments

Teacher/coach signature

Exercise

What do you wonder about? What are you curious about? Keep an ongoing list and explore a new item every month, or as you feel inspired...

'To do' list

Task/ Activity	Priority (A to F, where A = very important and F = unimportant

Monday

Tuesday

Wednesday

Thursday

Friday

Saturday

Sunday

It would take 100 years to watch every video on YouTube

Parent signature

Comments

Teacher/coach signature

Exercise

Pick an exercise from the list on page 148 – give it a try, then reflect on the experience and learning. What did you learn and enjoy while you were doing the task?

'To do' list

Task/ Activity	Priority (A to F, where A = very important and F = unimportant

Week
17

Monday

Tuesday

Wednesday

Thursday

Friday

Saturday

Sunday

Leadership is about creating an alignment of
strengths. making people's weaknesses irrelevant
PETER DRUCKER

Parent signature   Comments

Teacher/coach signature

Exercise

When you're feeling low and/ or upset, what do you do to move things forward?

'To do' list

Task/ Activity	Priority (A to F, where A = very important and F = unimportant

Monday

Tuesday

Wednesday

Thursday

Friday

Saturday

Sunday

The sloth moves so slowly that green algae grows in the grooves of their hair

Parent signature

Comments

Teacher/coach signature

Revisit your SOAR™
and review your achievements

Look at the SOAR™ diagram (page 10) you produced at the beginning of the journal and then answer the following questions:

Q1 Are you using your strengths more effectively?

Q2 What opportunities have you utilised and are there any more to engage with?

Q3 How are your aspirations being met and do they need updating?

Q4 What resources have you used and what have you achieved so far?

Finally, using the blank grid on the next page, update your SOAR™. You can also share it through social media or with people who can help and support you.

Well done – I'm sure things have moved on and this exercise provides an opportunity for a guided reflective experience...

Your personal SOAR™

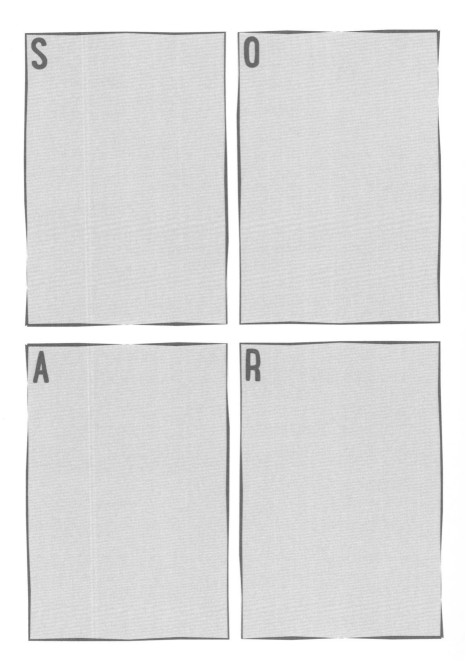

S

O

A

R

Monday

Tuesday

Wednesday

Thursday

Friday

Saturday

Sunday

Be the change you wish to see in the world
MAHATMA GANDHI

Parent signature

Comments

Teacher/coach signature

Exercise

Reflect on the exercise at the end of week 7 and draw up a list of the new things you've done. Write down what you notice about your achievements...

'To do' list

Task/ Activity	Priority (A to F, where A = very important and F = unimportant

Monday

Tuesday

Wednesday

Thursday

Friday

Saturday

Sunday

The colour blue has a calming effect. It causes
the brain to release calming hormones

Parent signature

Comments

Teacher/coach signature

Exercise

Select an activity or event you have coming up in the next week or two. Take five minutes and close your eyes and imagine it going perfectly. After the event, record how it's gone and see if you can notice any differences.

'To do' list

Task/ Activity	Priority (A to F, where A = very important and F = unimportant

Monday

Tuesday

Wednesday

Thursday

Friday

Saturday

Sunday

If you want to build a ship. don't drum up people to collect wood. and don't assign them tasks and work. but rather teach them to long for the vast and endless immensity of the sea.
ANTOINE DE SAINT-EXUPERY

Parent signature

Comments

Teacher/coach signature

Exercise

You've been doing the programme for a number of months. Have you noticed anything different in yourself? Any changes? What new things have you learned about yourself?

'To do' list

Task/ Activity	Priority (A to F, where A = very important and F = unimportant

Monday

Tuesday

Wednesday

Thursday

Friday

Saturday

Sunday

A slug has four noses ☀

Parent signature   Comments

Teacher/coach signature

Exercise

Pick an exercise from the list on page 148 – give it a try, then reflect on the experience and learning. What did you learn and enjoy while you were doing the task?

'To do' list

Task/ Activity	Priority (A to F, where A = very important and F = unimportant

Monday

Tuesday

Wednesday

Thursday

Friday

Saturday

Sunday

Do nothing. Time is too precious to waste.
BUDDHA

Parent signature

Comments

Teacher/coach signature

Exercise

Write down what's important about your friends and note down a few of the ways they help and support you...

'To do' list

Task/ Activity	Priority (A to F, where A = very important and F = unimportant

Week
24

Monday

Tuesday

Wednesday

Thursday

Friday

Saturday

Sunday

A giraffe can clean its ears with its own tongue

Parent signature

Comments

Teacher/coach signature

Exercise

Repeat the 'three good things' exercise.

'To do' list

Task/ Activity	Priority (A to F, where A = very important and F = unimportant

Monday

Tuesday

Wednesday

Thursday

Friday

Saturday

Sunday

Vision without action is a daydream.
Action without vision is a nightmare.
JAPANESE PROVERB

Parent signature

Comments

Teacher/coach signature

Exercise

Think of a relationship where you're experiencing difficulty. What things do you appreciate and value about this person and what can you learn from them?

'To do' list

Task/ Activity	Priority (A to F, where A = very important and F = unimportant

Week 26

Monday

Tuesday

Wednesday

Thursday

Friday

Saturday

Sunday

Add your favourite quote. joke or interesting fact and share it with your friends

---

Parent signature

Comments

Teacher/coach signature

Exercise

Write down the reasons your friends are important to you and then tell them why. Notice their reaction and record it here...

'To do' list

Task/ Activity	Priority (A to F, where A = very important and F = unimportant

Monday

Tuesday

Wednesday

Thursday

Friday

Saturday

Sunday

How can you make seven even?
Take away the letter 's'

Parent signature

Comments

Teacher/coach signature

Exercise

Pick an exercise from the list on page 148 – give it a try, then reflect on the experience and learning. What did you learn and enjoy while you were doing the task?

'To do' list

Task/ Activity	Priority (A to F, where A = very important and F = unimportant

Monday

Tuesday

Wednesday

Thursday

Friday

Saturday

Sunday

Happiness can be found even in the darkest times if only one remembers to turn on the light
ALBUS DUMBLEDORE IN HARRY POTTER AND THE PRISONER OF AZKABAN (SCREENPLAY BY STEVEN KLOVES)

Parent signature

Comments

Teacher/coach signature

Exercise

Look around you today and pay attention to the details: the colours of the leaves; designs of the buildings; the weather; the different ways people smile; the smells and sounds around you. What beauty can you find in the small things?

`To do` list

Task/ Activity	Priority (A to F, where A = very important and F = unimportant

Monday

Tuesday

Wednesday

Thursday

Friday

Saturday

Sunday

Do you have any invisible ink?
Certainly... what colour?

Parent signature

Comments

Teacher/coach signature

Exercise

Have you recently completed a really good project or piece of work? Ask yourself why it went well, why did this good thing happen, and 'how can I have more of it'?

'To do' list

Task/ Activity	Priority (A to F, where A = very important and F = unimportant

Monday

Tuesday

Wednesday

Thursday

Friday

Saturday

Sunday

What do you do if you see a spaceman?
Park your car man!

Parent signature   Comments

Teacher/coach signature

Exercise

When a project or piece of work hasn't gone as well as you'd hoped, ask yourself what you've learned and what you'd do differently?

'To do' list

Task/ Activity	Priority (A to F, where A = very important and F = unimportant

Monday

Tuesday

Wednesday

Thursday

Friday

Saturday

Sunday

Where does the General keep his armies?
Up his sleevies

Parent signature

Comments

Teacher/coach signature

Exercise

As you think of your average day, what makes you smile?

'To do' list

Task/ Activity	Priority (A to F, where A = very important and F = unimportant

Monday

Tuesday

Wednesday

Thursday

Friday

Saturday

Sunday

What do you call a friend who has an elephant on his head?
A flat mate

Parent signature   Comments

Teacher/coach signature

Exercise

Pick an exercise from the list on page 148 – give it a try, then write down your reflections and thinking on the experience and learning. What did you learn and enjoy?

'To do' list

Task/ Activity	Priority (A to F, where A = very important and F = unimportant

Monday

Tuesday

Wednesday

Thursday

Friday

Saturday

Sunday

Why is 6 afraid of 7?
Because 7 8 9

Parent signature

Comments

Teacher/coach signature

Exercise

Think of a time when you were in a leadership role...
What did you learn and notice?

'To do' list

Task/ Activity	Priority (A to F, where A = very important and F = unimportant

Monday

Tuesday

Wednesday

Thursday

Friday

Saturday

Sunday

What happened to the hungry clock?
It went back 4 seconds

Parent signature   Comments

Teacher/coach signature

Exercise

Repeat the 'three good things' exercise. Have you noticed any changes since you last did it?

'To do' list

Task/ Activity	Priority (A to F, where A = very important and F = unimportant

Monday

Tuesday

Wednesday

Thursday

Friday

Saturday

Sunday

Two eggs in a frying pan. One say 'it's hot in here'
the other says 'WOW... a talking egg!'

Parent signature

Comments

Teacher/coach signature

Exercise

Think of a tough time you've gone through.
Looking back, what have you learned and what
would you do differently now?

'To do' list

Task/ Activity	Priority (A to F, where A = very important and F = unimportant

Monday

Tuesday

Wednesday

Thursday

Friday

Saturday

Sunday

Never doubt that a small group of thoughtful,
committed citizens can change the world:
indeed, it's the only thing that ever has
MARGARET MEAD

Parent signature

Comments

Teacher/coach signature

Exercise

What's the best thing that has happened to you in the last seven days? Write it down as a story. Think about it for a few minutes and then notice the impact it has on you when you remember it...

'To do' list

Task/ Activity	Priority (A to F, where A = very important and F = unimportant

Monday

Tuesday

Wednesday

Thursday

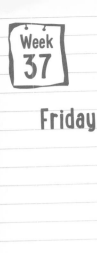

Friday

Saturday

Sunday

What do you call a pretend railway?
A play station

_____
Parent signature

Comments

_____
Teacher/coach signature

Exercise

Read through your journal and look at any of the drawings and comments. Try and notice any common trends and thoughts, then have a think to see if any thoughts come up. Write them as bullet points...

'To do' list

Task/ Activity	Priority (A to F, where A = very important and F = unimportant

Monday

Tuesday

Wednesday

Thursday

Friday

Saturday

Sunday

Creativity is putting your imagination to work, and it's
produced the most extraordinary results in human culture
KEN ROBINSON

Parent signature

Comments

Teacher/coach signature

Exercise

Well done, you've achieved a lot. Now record in your journal what you enjoyed, learned, achieved and valued...
Use images, words or pictures – anything that helps you understand the progress you've made.

`To do` list

Task/ Activity	Priority (A to F, where A = very important and F = unimportant

∽ PART FOUR ∽
Additional exercises

We've included the exercises that follow in a menu format, for you to use in addition to the weekly tasks, either on your own or in groups. If you're doing your journaling as a group activity, some of the tasks and exercises can be used as icebreakers and communication exercises.

Exercise 1:

Do something

Try to fit all three into your day:

★ Help someone
★ Get active outdoors
★ Take two minutes and just sit quietly, think and breathe

Exercise 2:

Thinking differently

This exercise is about engaging the creative part of your brain, opening it up to different possibilities.

★ Find someone to work with, and agree which one of you is **A** and who's going to be **B**
★ **A** asks the three questions below, allocating about three minutes per question (total nine minutes per person).
★ When **B** has answered them all, change over
★ Practice not interrupting or following up with questions – try and listen very carefully without adding your story!

Q1: Share something you really enjoyed in your childhood or early life – something that stood out for you. Tell it as a story...

Q2: What is the one thing you do that you really enjoy doing?

Q3: In all your life experiences so far, what one thing caused you to go 'WOW'? (It can be small or major and very simple... A beautiful view, a great YouTube clip or a great sporting moment, for example)

Exercise 3:

Mindfulness

Find out more about mindfulness and its benefits and try one of the exercises, then record the experience in your journal.

Exercise 4:

Ten new things to have a go at in 100 days

This task is about taking some risks, operating out of your comfort zone.

The interesting thing is that, for some people, what seems a simple task for others is a very challenging one. One example is picking up a spider – for some it means nothing whereas for others it's a major problem.

The task is to think about and draw up ten activities or actions that are a challenge for you, or something you've always wanted to do. It could be a ride at a funfair; it could be learning a musical instrument; visiting a place you've always wanted to; or doing something that scares you.

Draw up the list and then get on with them. Each time you do one of them write it up in your journal. Reflect on the experience and what it taught you. Record your success using train tickets, selfies, receipts, entry passes (you can use an app that frames the object) – upload them on your social media page or stick them in your journal.

1.

2.

3.

4.

5.

6.

7.

8.

9.

10.

Exercise 5:

Share something

Using your Facebook page, or other social media platform, upload:

★ Positive images of people and situations that affected you
★ Things you are doing well
★ Actions your friends and family have taken to support you and your thanks
★ What you have recently achieved

Exercise 6:

Friendship tasks

In Love 2.0 Barbara Fredrickson (see the appendix on page 158) writes about 'finding happiness and health in moments of connection and of shared positivity. Even micro-moments of genuine connection make you healthier, and being healthier builds your capacity for love,' she says. Take a moment to think of a time in the last few days when you felt connected with someone or something and appreciate them and your role in that connection.

★ Think of a friendship that you have, or choose a friendship that you have seen in your own circle (or on screen). Write down three things that you like about that friendship...

★ Write down three things that you like about yourself as a friend...

★ Send an email or use a Facebook comment to thank a friend and tell them what you enjoy about the relationship.

Exercise 7:

Creating a gift

Make a small gift for a friend or family member – it could be a meal, a cake, an invitation to share a special activity or a piece of art/craft. Don't forget to record it and the reaction.

Exercise 8:

Talking stick

This is a simple two-person exercise that is both fun and helps you have better conversations with people. It uses a 'talking stick.' This is an ancient way to help all people in a group feel able to speak without fear of challenge, allowing people to listen more. For this task you will need a simple object that can be used as a talking piece – it can be a ring, a coin a pencil or small pebble, for example.

The rules are simple – place the talking stick between the two of you. The person asking the question picks it up and asks the question, then puts it down again. The person answering the questions then picks it up, answers the question, and then puts it down. Whoever holds the talking piece is the only person who can speak.

Find someone to do this with – agree who's **A** and who is **B** and then use the talking piece. **A** will first ask a simple question; they need to be short and could be about personal interests like favourite films, colours or food. **B** answers the question using no more than three words.

The exercise should be undertaken at a fast pace, and there should be no interruptions or clarifications. After five minutes change roles...

When it's finished, have a conversation about what happened and what you noticed. Record your reactions in your journal. Think about the challenges of answering the questions in a few words.

Exercise 9:

Give something away

All of us have too much 'stuff'. Give something away – it could be to a friend, charity shop or to someone who needs it...

Exercise 10:

Stone balancing

Stone balancing creates beautiful images, where rocks are balanced on top of one another in various positions. There are no tricks involved to aid in the balancing, like adhesives, wires or supports. It can be a performance art, a spectacle, or period of dedicated concentration – depending upon the interpretation by the artist or audience. Choosing the rocks and finding the balance point require patience and sensitivity.

It helps us see that the physical world is not as fixed as we might think. http://en.wikipedia.org/wiki/Rock_balancing.

Here's a short video illustrating an artist at work: http://www.youtube.com/watch?v=-wYpV3MNT28.

Next time you're out, have a go at balancing a couple of rocks – or collect some to try it at home. Treat it like a meditation where the goal is not important. http://www.youtube.com/watch?v=-hmKNNTT_CE.

Exercise 11:

Make someone laugh

Cheer a friend up with a joke – if you're stuck, try some of the examples we've used in the journal!

Exercise 12:

Different uses of a ruler

Here's a task to get your creative head going – assemble a small group of friends and divide them into two teams. Using a ruler, brainstorm the maximum variety of uses. The winning team is the one with the most – and also the most creative and off the wall – these might be the ones that make you laugh.

After the exercise, record the personal effect on you and the participants. What was interesting and how did it make you feel? Can you beat the 64 variations created by our original group of Studio School students?

Exercise 13:

Volunteer

Either by yourself, or with friends, do some volunteering. It could be something in your community like a small environmental project or fundraising for a local charity.

Exercise 14:

Creating a gift

Make a small gift for a friend or family member – it could be a meal, a cake, an invitation to share a special activity or a piece of art/craft. Don't forget to record it and the reaction.

Reflective exercises

1. Whatever you focus on grows... Remember that where we choose to put our attention has an effect, so by focusing on something we like or want we can see more opportunities to bring it into our life. Focusing on negatives causes them to figure more largely in our awareness and absorb our energy. What do you want more of in your life right now and how can you shift more of your attention to it?

2. Sometimes our thinking can distract us from the present moment. Take a few moments today to do nothing, by simply sitting with your eyes closed...

3. Focus on your breathing and let your mind go blank. What are you aware of and how do you feel afterwards?

PART FIVE
Guidance and useful information

Part five includes information on the methodologies that have influenced our content.

This information is included to help teachers and parents working with young people to understand the methodologies behind some of the ideas and theories we've introduced.

How to be More Awesome: the student planner edition is based upon the Appreciating People journals How to be More Awesome and Food for Thought. These journals were developed as a learning resource and personal development tool. Its purpose is to support people to be more resilient, to build on their personal strengths and to be more aware and appreciative of the world around them.

For teachers and young people interested in the methodology behind the Awesome journal, here's some useful guidance and information...

Positive psychology

Positive Psychology is the scientific study of positive aspects of human life, such as happiness, wellbeing and flourishing. It looks at how these qualities develop and grow and how we can maintain them.

Professor Martin Seligman is the founding father of Positive Psychology and a major figure in the wellbeing movement. He believes that a happier society requires us to pay more attention to the quality of our inner life, and to use proven methods to improve it. That is what Positive Psychology is about – it goes beyond the treatment of depression and anxiety to ways we could all lead more rewarding lives.

The exercises and approach it offers include the systematic practice of kindness, gratitude to others, counting your blessings and exploiting your strengths rather than attacking your weaknesses. It also teaches resilience and optimism.

Positive Psychology is one of the newest branches of psychology – the first World Congress was held in 2009.

Some Positive Psychology research findings:

★ People are generally happy
★ Money does not necessarily buy wellbeing: but spending money on other people does
★ Some of the best ways to combat disappointments and setbacks include social relationships and character strengths
★ Work can be important to wellbeing, especially when people are able to engage in work that is purposeful and meaningful
★ While happiness is influenced by genetics, people can learn to be happier by developing optimism, gratitude and altruism.

Have you ever wondered why the world seems more inclusive and open when you're in a good mood, and why your circumstances seem so narrow when you're feeling down? How can you nurture the good feelings so they last longer and have more powerful effects on your life?

Dr Barbara Fredrickson is an author *(Positivity and Love 2.0)* and leading scholar in the area of Positive Psychology. Her 'broaden-and-build' theory explains why positive emotions change your perspective on life and how they can help you develop valuable emotional resources, like resilience and mindfulness. She has found, in over 20 years of research, that individuals need to keep a certain ratio of positive emotions to negative ones in order to flourish.

The video **Positive Emotions Open Our Mind** highlights her work – you can watch it on YouTube: http://www.youtube.com/watch?v=Z7dFDHzV36g.

Take some time to watch the YouTube film, and a few moments to reflect. Then record your thoughts and ideas.

Three particularly notable things about positive emotions are:

★ **They help us be more open. For example, a number of experiments have been done where giving students a gift of sweets before an exam helps them feel more positive before they start and they then do better in the exam**

★ **They help people find better 'win-win' solutions**

★ **They help people be more resilient**

It's interesting to note over 60 UK schools are now using Positive Psychology approaches (see Action for Happiness). Martin Seligman and his colleagues at Penn State University have developed a range of wellbeing programmes for schools, the military and hospitals.

Look at the Canadian Positive Psychology Association Vimeo film on introducing three good things into a primary school at www.vimeo.com100393013. Any thoughts on the film?

Mindfulness

Have you ever opened a bag of crisps or a bar of chocolate, and found that you have eaten it all in a flash while watching a screen, without realising exactly what you have been doing?

More people are beginning to understand that having our 'minds full' of things to do or worry about is not good for us. Being 'mindful' – even just for two minutes at a time – helps our mind and bodies to relax.

Jon Kabat-Zinn is a famous teacher of mindfulness meditation. His definition of mindfulness is: 'Mindfulness means paying attention in a particular way; on purpose, in the present moment, and non-judgmentally.'

Appreciative Inquiry

Central to this journal is the organisational and community development process called Appreciative Inquiry (AI). The term 'appreciative' comes from the idea that when something increases in value it 'appreciates'.

'Inquiry' describes the process of seeking to understand through questions and the value of paying attention to the things that, if increased, would add value and make a difference.

AI is the cousin of Positive Psychology and part of the growing movement to focus on and build from the strengths and assets of people and groups. By working from this positive focus (as opposed to focusing on what's not working) people become more resilient and creative. They develop and deliver success and achieve realistic solutions to problems.

First developed by David Cooperrider in the late 1980s at Case Western University in the USA, it's now used all over the world by large and small organisations, communities, villages, and in personal development programmes. Significant contribution to the practical application of AI was made by Jane Magruder Watkins

A useful definition –

'AI is a process for engaging people in building the kinds of organisations and a world they want to live in. Working from people's strengths and positive experiences, AI co-creates a future based on collaboration and dialogue'

David Cooperrider

It's important to remember that AI is not about positive thinking, but about how we both individually and collectively create change; it's not about ignoring problems, but looking at them differently.

More information about Appreciative Inquiry and its application can be found on www.appreciatingpeople.co.uk and www.bemoreawesome.net and Appreciative Inquiry Commons www.appreciatinginquiry.case.edu.

Within the Appreciative Inquiry approach there are three tools:

★ Appreciative conversation frameworks – these are a set of structured questions to help us inquire more deeply into a topic – for example 'friendship' or 'working together'. These structured conversations are used to discover the strengths of people and organisations, and 'what works'.

★ A useful framework for projects and programmes called the **5D process**: The Ds – definition (what are we going to look at?); discovery (finding out what works and existing assets); dream (imagining what could be); design (determining what needs to be done) and delivery/ destiny (how are we going to do it?) – are used to help us structure projects.

★ SOAR™ (strengths, opportunities, aspirations and results/ resources, are described on page nine). It's a simple framework for both strategic planning and personal development.

SOAR is trademarked and was created by Jackie Stavros and Gina Hinrichs (have a look at *The Thin Book of SOAR: building strength-based strategy,* 2009). A useful web site is www.soar-strategy.com.

Alongside a model for organisational and community development, AI has contributed to different approaches in mentoring, coaching, forward-planning, leadership, team building, counselling and international development. To learn more, have a look at the reading list and surf the internet for AI examples and articles as well as the suggested web sites above.

Ten keys to happier living - your 'Great Dream'

Action for Happiness describe **Ten Keys to Happier Living** that can make people's lives happier and more fulfilling: 'GREAT DREAM'. The first five keys (GREAT) are about how we interact with the **outside** world in our daily activities – based on the **nef** Five Ways to Wellbeing.

The second five keys (DREAM) come from **inside** us and depend on our attitude to life. These ten keys bring together many of the things we have talked about already.

G iving
R elating
E xercising
A ppreciating
T rying out

D irection
R elating
E motion
A cceptance
M eaning

www.actionforhappiness.org/10-keys-to-happier-living

Next steps

We have created www.bemoreawesome.net – a website for you to upload any journal comments on the tasks and exercises you've completed. This site will also provide additional information on journaling, wellbeing and guidance on journaling workshops and support.

If you're interested in learning more about Appreciative Living, Appreciative Inquiry and Positive Psychology, we recommend you visit www.appreciativeliving.com and our site at www.appreciatingpeople. co.uk.

Final advice – keep journaling and working at it.

Acknowledgements

Thanks to all the people who have helped – this resource couldn't have been produced without the support and guidance of a number people

We have drawn a lot from the work of the pioneers of Positive Psychology and the freely available material on the web which has allowed it to spread and grow – thank you to everyone who has contributed to that work. Much appreciation is also due to the generous and inspired AI practitioners worldwide whose work has guided and influenced us. A special mention goes to Jackie Kelm for allowing us to use her Appreciative Living work and many of her great questions.

Appreciating People

Appreciating People works with people, communities, businesses, charities and organisations to help them get the best out of themselves and are leading UK experts in the use of AI. We work regionally, nationally and internationally from our base in Liverpool, UK. More information available at www.appreciatingpeople.co.uk.

Northern Schools Trust

The Studio opened in September 2013 to provide a new type of education for 14 to 19 year olds. Alongside GCSE, A Levels and BTEC qualifications, students prepare for employment in the digital and creative sectors by following a programme of project-based learning mentored by partners from the sector. In addition to these skills, Northern Schools Trust's emphasis is on developing students who are self-aware and skilled at building relationships so they can develop positive mindsets that are essential for digital leaders. www.thestudioliverpool.uk

The Northern Schools Trust is a charitable trust that works specifically in areas of social and economic deprivation to transform the lives of children and young people through education. The Trust currently works with a small selection of home-grown, innovative academies in the North West of England. www.northernschoolstrust.co.uk

Holly Langley

Holly is an artist/designer who lives in Liverpool. Her background is in TV, theatre and community arts. She generates artwork with people in schools, community groups, art organisations and theatres. Holly is an illustrator, painter and maker. She is an active part of 'More Than Minutes', a collective of illustrators who create visual minutes live at events.

Wordscapes

Wordscapes are storytellers and award-winning non-fiction publishers. Based in Liverpool, they work with clients locally, nationally and internationally, publishing a range of traditional books alongside eBooks and magazines, creating web content and making films. For more information about their work, have a look at www.wordscape.org.uk.

How to be More Awesome:
the student planner edition

Written by Tim Slack and Suzanne Quinney
Design and production: Ken Ashcroft
Illustrations: Holly Langley
Editor: Fiona Shaw

Printed and bound in the UK by Printfine Ltd.

ISBN: 978-0-9930221-9-7

First published in September 2016 by
Wordscapes Ltd.
Second Floor,
Elevator Studios
27 Parliament Street
Liverpool L8 5RN
www.wordscape.org.uk

www.bemoreawesome.net